99 Day Spiritual Cleanse

Return to Your Light

Isaiah A. Tisdale

An Imprint of tbudget, LLC 744 South Street #997
Philadelphia, PA 19147

Copyright © 2020 by Isaiah A. Tisdale

All rights reserved.No part of this book may be reproduced in any form or by any electronic or mechanical means, including information storage and retrieval systems, without written permission from the author, except for the use of brief quotations in a book review. For information address tbudget, LLC, 744 South Street #997, Philadelphia, PA 19147.

First tbudget trade paperback edition January 2020

Printed in the United States of America

Library of Congress Control Number: 2021901600
ISBN: 978-1-7346351-5-7 (Paperback)
ISBN: 978-1-7346351-6-4 (eBook)

http://www.isaiahatisdale.com

Contents

Introduction

Part One: *Connect to your flow of energy*

Root Chakra

Root Chakra Pose Instructions

Sacral Chakra

Sacral Chakra Pose Instructions

Part Two: *Recognize any disruption in your energy flow*

Sacral Chakra

Solar Plexus Chakra

Solar Plexus Chakra Pose Instructions

Part Three: *Observe the disruption*

Solar Plexus Chakra

Heart Chakra

Heart Chakra Pose Instructions

Throat Chakra

Throat Chakra Pose Instructions

Part Four: *Surrender your hold on the negative energy flow*

Throat Chakra

Third Eye Chakra

Third Eye Chakra Pose Instructions

Part Five: *Affirm high-frequency energy in your life*

Third Eye Chakra

Crown Chakra

Crown Chakra Pose Instructions

Closing

About the Author

Introduction

I wholeheartedly believe that we are far more powerful in our wholeness than in our fragmentation. Many ask, *how do we become whole?* The answer is simple, yet profound: through continuous healing. Over time, we are conditioned and shaped by external influences that pull us away from our true selves. This process of domestication creates disconnection—from our truth, our purpose, and our inner power.

Through my own healing journey, I have experienced transformative shifts within my mind, body, and spirit. These shifts awakened me to my purpose in the Universe and deepened my understanding of what it means to live in alignment. This awakening is not reserved for a few—it is available to all. And through this work, my intention is to support you as you reconnect with your own truth.

In 2021, I felt called to expand my healing energy and empower others to begin their own inner work. I came to understand that energetic balance is essential for a fulfilling and aligned life. The frequency of our lives is shaped by the energy we carry, and that energy is a direct reflection of our healing. The question then becomes: *how do you begin to heal your inner world?*

This book is an invitation to that process. It is designed to help you release energetic blockages, reconnect with your natural state, and return to a life rooted in awareness, unconditional love, and harmony. Healing your inner world is not separate from your outer experience—it is the foundation of it. As you transform within, that transformation flows into every area of your life.

At the core of this journey are the energy centers within

you—the chakras—which guide the flow of your life force. Each chakra holds its own wisdom, challenges, and opportunities for growth. In this book, we will explore each of the seven chakras and uncover ways to release stagnant or negative energy, allowing your natural flow to be restored.

Your connection to your mind, body, and spirit determines the frequency you operate in. Your mind holds your thoughts and emotions, and it is through conscious awareness and healing that you can release trauma and restore balance. When your energy flows freely, you return to a state of alignment, clarity, and peace.

This is a process of remembering who you are beyond conditioning and ego. It is a journey of releasing unconscious patterns and stepping into awareness. The ego thrives in separation and fear, but your truth exists in unity and love.

As you move through this book, my intention is that you dig deep, reflect honestly, and free yourself from the captivity of unconsciousness. This is not a journey you take alone—we are connected, and our shared awareness strengthens the collective.

Darkness is not the enemy—it is simply the absence of light. Light is love, and fear dissolves in its presence. When you choose to shine your light on your fears, you begin to transform them. And through that transformation, you evolve.

This is your invitation to return to yourself, to reclaim your power, and to live in alignment with your highest truth.

What are chakras?
Chakras are energy centers in your body.

What are chakras connected to in the body?

Root:
base of the spine, legs, feet, bones, large intestine, colon, and adrenal glands

Sacral:
lower abdomen, reproductive system, bladder, sexual organs, and kidneys.

Solar plexus:
upper abdomen, stomach, liver, pancreas, small intestine, gallbladder, and muscular system

Heart:
heart, lungs, rib cage, arms, hands, circulatory system, and thymus gland

Throat:
throat, neck, jaw, mouth, vocal cords, and thyroid gland

Third Eye:
brain, eyes, ears, nose, nervous system, sinuses, and pineal gland

Crown:
top of the head, brain, nervous system, and pituitary gland

What are some indicators of chakra imbalance?
I've outlined the chakras and the barriers that may affect their balance.

Chakras

Crown Chakra	🟣	Barriers: attachment, awareness, and connection to the Divine
Third Eye Chakra	🔵	Barriers: inner balance, intuition, and meaning
Throat Chakra	🟢	Barriers: communication, lies, and truth
Heart Chakra	🟢	Barriers: anger, grief, forgiveness, and love
Solar Plexus Chakra	🟡	Barriers: anxiety, power, purpose, and shame
Sacral Chakra	🟠	Barriers: creativity, guilt, and sexuality
Root Chakra	🟠	Barriers: fear, groundedness, and survival

Through your cleanse, please remember:

To breathe.
This practice is essential to both your mantras and yoga poses. Become the observer of your breath—notice its rhythm and the impact it has on your body. Breathwork is the fifth element of this cleanse, and the most powerful.

Be honest.
This intention is essential as you engage with the questions and process your thoughts and feelings. Release judgment—allow everything to flow freely, whether in your mind or onto the page. A journal becomes a powerful space for honesty and self-acceptance when you allow it.

Let go!
This embodiment is essential to the cleanse. Release the need for "correctness" in your thoughts, words, or actions. Trust what feels liberating to your soul, and let go of anything that no longer serves your growth.

Step One:
Connect to your flow of energy

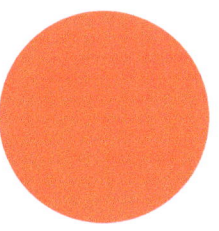

Root Chakra

The root chakra is the foundation of your being—grounding you in stability, connection to nature, and the lessons of life. Your beliefs, sense of security, and loyalty all shape the strength of this energy center.

When imbalanced, disruptions may arise in areas such as safety, security, basic needs, trust, and alignment with social or family beliefs. These imbalances can manifest not only emotionally, but physically, often presenting as tension in the lower back or feelings of heaviness and depression.

When balanced, the root chakra anchors you in strength and presence. You become grounded, self-aware, and rooted in self-mastery. Abundance becomes visible in all aspects of life, and your energy flows with stability, resilience, and positivity.

As you move through the mantras and yoga poses connected to this chakra, take at least **<u>four</u>** deep, intentional breaths—inhaling fully and exhaling with awareness—to deepen your connection and restore balance.

Root Chakra Pose Instructions

- **Half-moon pose** – balance on one leg, extend the opposite leg and arm, and open your chest to the side.
- **Child's pose** – kneel, sit back on your heels, and lower your torso forward with arms extended or relaxed.
- **Elephant pose** – stand wide, fold forward, squat low, and bring your forearms between your legs with hands rising toward your forehead.
- **Crescent low lunge pose** – step one foot forward, lower the back knee, and lift your torso with arms reaching up.
- **Knee-to-chest pose** – lie on your back and gently pull one or both knees into your chest.
- **Bound angle pose** – sit tall, bring the soles of your feet together, and let your knees fall open.
- **Mountain pose** – stand tall with feet grounded, arms at your sides, and spine aligned.
- **Tree pose** – balance on one leg, place the other foot on your inner leg, and bring hands to heart or overhead.
- **Frog pose** – lower to your forearms and widen your knees, keeping hips aligned with knees.

Root Chakra Pose Instructions

- **Warrior II pose** – step wide, bend your front knee, and extend arms parallel to the ground.
- **Wide-legged forward fold pose** – stand with legs wide and fold forward, bringing hands toward the floor.
- **Garland pose** – squat low with feet grounded and bring hands together at your heart.
- **Easy pose** – sit cross-legged with a tall spine and relaxed shoulders.
- **Standing forward fold pose** – fold forward from standing, letting your head and arms relax toward the ground.
- **Locust pose** – lie on your belly and lift your chest, arms, and legs off the ground.

DAY 1

mantra

I am worthy of all that flows to me.

words of wisdom

Trust is a sacred foundation of your reality. When you trust yourself and the Divine order of life, you allow light to enter every space you occupy. Nothing is out of place—everything is unfolding as it should. Release doubt, as it weakens your connection to truth, and instead choose faith in your role within the Universe. When you trust your participation, you strengthen your relationships, your path, and your inner stability.

yoga pose

Half-moon pose

questions for introspection

Do you trust yourself fully? Do you trust others? What early experiences shaped your view of trust, and how can you begin to rebuild it from a place of strength and awareness?

DAY 2

mantra
I am energized and alive in my body.

words of wisdom

Honor your truth above all illusions. Shame is not your identity—it is a learned response that drains your energy and disconnects you from your power. What you may have once labeled as mistakes are truly opportunities to refine your boundaries and deepen your self-respect. Move with integrity in your thoughts, actions, and expression. When you live honorably, you reclaim your energy and stand firmly in your worth.

yoga pose

Child pose

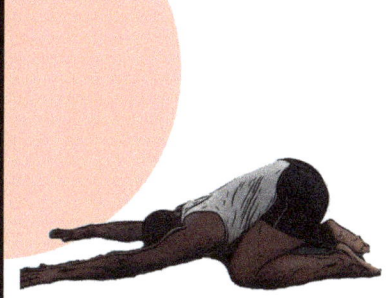

questions for introspection
What do you truly honor in your life? In what ways have your actions aligned—or misaligned—with what you value most?

DAY 3

mantra
I am balanced in mind, body, and spirit.

words of wisdom

Balance is essential for stability and grounding. Life may attempt to pull you into chaos through distraction, but you always have the ability to return to your center. There is ease available to you when you choose alignment over overwhelm. Do not hold back from creating a life that feels balanced and supportive. When you honor equilibrium, you empower yourself to move through life with clarity and intention.

yoga pose

Elephant pose

questions for introspection
Do you feel grounded and supported in your life? What practices, environments, or habits would help you feel more rooted and secure?

DAY 4

mantra
I am strong and rooted in my foundation.

words of wisdom

The Universe is always working in your favor, even when it is not immediately clear. Challenges are not punishments—they are opportunities for growth and expansion across all aspects of your being. Refuse to take on the role of a victim. Instead, observe, learn, and evolve. Every experience is guiding you toward a stronger, wiser, and more grounded version of yourself.

yoga pose

Crescent low lunge pose

questions for introspection
Do you believe life is working in your favor? Where do you feel like a victim to your circumstances? What would shift if you chose to see every experience as part of your growth and Divine order?

DAY 5

mantra
I am essential to Divine order and purpose.

words of wisdom

You are placed exactly where you need to be. Your role in life is intentional and significant. While you are born into a family, you are not confined by it—you have the power to define what family means for you. If your environment does not align with your values, you are allowed to create new spaces that do. Set boundaries with clarity and confidence, and honor the connections that support your truth.

yoga pose

Knee-to-chest pose

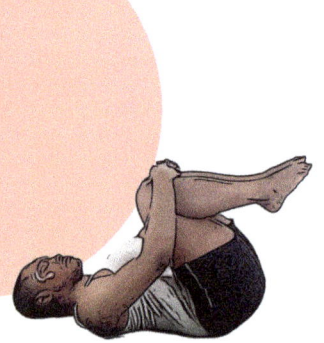

questions for introspection
How have your family dynamics shaped your sense of self? Identify three relationships that feel emotionally heavy—how can you begin to release, redefine, or set boundaries to support your healing?

DAY 6

mantra
I am secure within myself and my path.

words of wisdom

Your safety is sacred, and you are your own protector. You have the authority to guard your energy, your space, and your well-being. Self-security begins within, and it sets the standard for what you allow into your life. Any past violations or experiences do not define your present—they serve as catalysts for your transformation. Stand firmly in your power and protect what is sacred to you.

yoga pose

Bound angle pose

questions for introspection
In what ways do you feel unsafe or unsupported—physically, emotionally, mentally, or spiritually? What steps can you take to strengthen your sense of security and protection?

DAY 7

mantra
I am resilient and rise through all experiences.

words of wisdom

Attachment can limit your spiritual expansion. You are not dependent on anything outside of yourself to experience joy, fulfillment, or peace. Life is meant to be experienced, not clung to. When you release attachment, you open yourself to freedom and deeper presence. Embrace impermanence and trust that you are whole, regardless of what comes and goes.

yoga pose

Mountain pose

questions for introspection
What attachments do you currently hold onto? How would your life feel without them? How can you begin to release dependency while still appreciating what they bring?

DAY 8

mantra

I am centered, grounded, and present.

words of wisdom

Your past does not dictate your peace. Early conditioning may have shaped your reactions, but it does not have to define your reality. As a conscious being, you have the power to unlearn, to shift, and to reclaim your inner calm. Do not allow past environments to block your access to tranquility. Choose awareness, choose grounding, and choose peace.

yoga pose

Tree pose

questions for introspection

What grounding words did you need to hear as a child? Does your inner child still need that reassurance? How can you intentionally support and nurture your inner child today?

DAY 9

mantra
I am safe and protected in all that I do.

words of wisdom

You are free to be your authentic self. You are not bound by inherited fears, limitations, or unconscious patterns. Even if you were once made to feel restricted, that is no longer your truth. You are protected, guided, and fully capable of leading your life with independence and confidence. Step into your freedom and reclaim your authority.

yoga pose

Frog pose

questions for introspection
How have your family's beliefs influenced your ability to live authentically? What beliefs are yours, and what beliefs are ready to be released?

DAY 10

mantra

I am aligned with financial abundance and stability.

words of wisdom

Abundance is a frequency that begins within you. Money is not scarce—it flows where intention, awareness, and alignment exist. When your relationship with money is rooted in clarity rather than ego, you remove blockages from your mind, body, and spirit. Cultivate practices that support financial stability, and trust that you are a magnet for abundance.

yoga pose

Warrior II pose

questions for introspection

How are you currently supporting your financial well-being? What habits or practices can you strengthen to create more stability and abundance?

DAY 11

mantra
I am thriving in perfect health and vitality.

words of wisdom

Your body is the foundation of your existence. It carries you, supports you, and allows you to fulfill your purpose. Caring for your physical health is not optional—it is essential. When you nurture both your inner and outer body, you deepen your awareness and strengthen your presence. Listen to your body, honor its needs, and respect the vessel that sustains you.

yoga pose

Wide-legged forward fold pose

questions for introspection
How would you describe your current physical health? What intentional changes can you make to better support your body and vitality?

DAY 12

mantra
I am fearless in the face of the unknown.

words of wisdom

Stand firmly in your values without fear. Others may project their limitations onto you, but their fear is not your truth. When you honor your values consistently, you activate a powerful alignment within yourself. This alignment attracts intentional energy and supports your higher self. Do not shrink—expand into your truth with confidence.

yoga pose

Garland pose

questions for introspection
What values do you stand by in this present moment? Which values no longer align with who you are becoming?

DAY 13

mantra

I am stable and supported in every step.

words of wisdom

You are allowed to evolve beyond tradition. What has been passed down is not always meant to be carried forward unchanged. You have the power to question, redefine, and create new ways of living. Respect what resonates, release what does not, and remain open to transformation. Growth requires both courage and grounding—embody both.

yoga pose

Easy pose

questions for introspection

What does tradition mean to you? How can you create or redefine traditions that reflect your truth and values?

DAY 14

mantra
I am brave in honoring my truth.

words of wisdom

Nature is your natural source of grounding and restoration. It offers stillness, clarity, and a deep sense of connection. Fear may have distanced you from it, but nature is not your enemy—it is your ally. Step outside, reconnect, and allow yourself to be supported by the Earth. In nature, you remember who you are.

yoga pose

Standing forward fold pose

questions for introspection
How connected are you to nature? What steps can you take to deepen your relationship with the natural world and ground your energy?

DAY 15

mantra
I am content and fulfilled with all that I have.

words of wisdom

Honor yourself without hesitation. External validation is temporary, but self-recognition is everlasting. Everything you seek—peace, love, fulfillment—already exists within you. When you acknowledge your own greatness, you unlock a deeper level of power and contentment. Affirm yourself daily and allow your inner light to expand without limits.

yoga pose

Locust pose

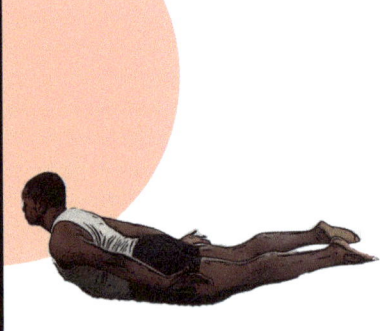

questions for introspection
The root chakra is represented by the number four. What are 44 qualities you admire about yourself, and how do they reflect your strength, stability, and foundation?

Sacral Chakra

The sacral chakra governs connection, experience, and emotional flow. It influences how you relate to others, engage with life, and embrace new experiences. Your sexuality, sense of well-being, creativity, feelings of abundance, and ability to make aligned choices are all rooted in this energy center.

When imbalanced, disruptions may arise around fear, control, power, intimacy, pleasure, and money. These imbalances can also manifest physically in the lower back, bladder, or pelvic region, and emotionally as disconnection from joy.

When balanced, the sacral chakra supports creativity, emotional awareness, and meaningful connection. You move with openness, compassion, and a natural flow of passion, pleasure, and inspiration.

As you move through the mantras and yoga poses connected to this chakra, take at least **<u>three</u>** deep, intentional breaths—inhaling fully and exhaling with awareness—to restore flow and deepen your connection.

Sacral Chakra Pose Instructions

- **Moonflowers pose** – stand tall with arms raised in a V-shape, palms facing forward and fingers spread wide.
- **Three-legged dog pose** – from downward dog pose, lift one leg high while keeping hips aligned.
- **Horse pose** – step wide, bend your knees, and lower into a squat with your torso upright.
- **Triangle pose** – extend one arm down to your leg or floor and the other upward, opening your chest.
- **Goddess pose** – stand wide, bend your knees outward, and raise your arms into a strong, open stance.
- **Supine spinal twist pose** – lie on your back, drop your knees to one side, and turn your gaze opposite.
- **Seated side stretch pose** – sit tall, extend one arm overhead, and lean gently to the side.
- **Wide-angle seated forward bend pose** – sit with legs wide and fold forward, reaching toward the floor.
- **Half lord of the fishes pose** – sit, cross one leg over the other, and twist your torso toward the bent knee.
- **Seated forward bend pose** – sit with legs extended and fold forward, reaching toward your feet.

Sacral Chakra Pose Instructions

- **Sphinx pose** – lie on your belly, lift your chest, and support yourself on your forearms.
- **Cobra pose** – press into your hands and lift your chest while keeping hips grounded.
- **Bow pose** – lie on your belly, grab your ankles, and lift your chest and legs upward.
- **Eagle pose** – balance on one leg, wrap the other leg and arms, and sit into a focused stance.

DAY 16

mantra

I feel like the source of nourishing, fruitful relationships.

words of wisdom

Relationships are multidimensional, reflecting both your inner world and external reality. Your relationship with money is one expression of this, shaping how you experience abundance and security. Money is not your power—you are. When the ego attaches to it, imbalance follows. Release control, embody abundance, and recognize there is always more than enough. In this alignment, money becomes a tool, not something that governs you.

yoga pose

Moonflowers pose

questions for introspection

What is your current relationship with money? Do you associate money with power? If so, where does that belief come from, and how can you redefine power as something that comes from within?

DAY 17

mantra
I feel in control of my life, trusting my power to choose.

words of wisdom

Let go. The desire to control everything is rooted in fear of the unknown and the ego's need for certainty. While you are empowered in your own life and guided by Divine energy, you are not meant to control people, outcomes, or timing. Redirect your energy inward, where your true power resides. When you release external control, you create space to reconnect with your authentic self and move through life with trust and flow.

yoga pose

Three-legged dog pose

questions for introspection
Do you feel a strong need to control outcomes, people, or situations? How does this show up in your daily life? What would shift if you surrendered control and trusted Divine flow?

DAY 18

mantra

I feel sensual, magnetic, and embodied in my essence.

words of wisdom

Your sexual energy is sacred, creative, and deeply transformative. When you honor it, you clear energetic blockages and restore balance within your being. There is freedom in fully embracing your sexuality without shame or hesitation, regardless of external acceptance. Your journey is personal—allow yourself to explore what feels aligned, satisfying, and true to your soul. In doing so, you deepen your connection with yourself and your creative life force.

yoga pose

Horse pose

questions for introspection

How comfortable are you with your sexuality? Do you allow yourself to express it freely and authentically, or do you hold back? Why?

DAY 19

mantra
I feel patient and aligned with Divine timing.

words of wisdom

Do not dim your inspiration by placing it on hold. There is no "perfect time" to begin—Divine timing is always present and active. When you delay your ideas, you disconnect from your creative momentum. Continue to inspire yourself, take intentional action, and trust that your efforts will unfold as they are meant to. Patience is not passive—it is trusting the process while continuing to move forward.

yoga pose

Triangle pose

questions for introspection
What truly inspires you? How can you nurture that inspiration and allow it to fuel your passion and daily actions?

DAY 20

mantra

I feel creative and in flow with Universal energy.

words of wisdom

Your creative nature is limitless, yet fear can silence its expression. Within you are ideas meant to bring light, impact, and transformation into the Universe. When an idea arises, do not judge or suppress it. Instead, nurture it with intention, take aligned action, and allow it to evolve naturally. You are a creator—trust your ability to bring your visions into reality.

yoga pose

Goddess pose

questions for introspection

Do you recognize yourself as a creative being? What ideas live within you, and how can you begin to use them to create transformation in your life?

DAY 21

mantra
I feel joyful from within.

words of wisdom

The belief in lack is an illusion created by the unconscious mind. In truth, you already hold access to what you need, often before you even realize it. When you shift into an abundant mindset, you release limitation and open yourself to receiving with ease. There is comfort and power in understanding that nothing is missing—everything is already within reach.

yoga pose

Supine spinal twist pose

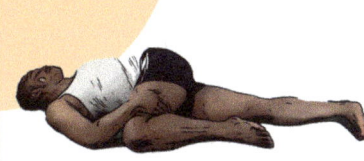

questions for introspection
What does abundance mean to you on a deeper level? Do you feel abundant now, or are you waiting for something external to create that feeling?

DAY 22

mantra
I feel emotionally balanced and at peace.

words of wisdom

Your emotions are powerful reflections of your inner world. The energy they carry can either expand your awareness or create imbalance if left unchecked. When you cultivate awareness and emotional balance, you gain mastery over your responses. Practices like conscious breathing help you return to peace, regulate your energy, and maintain clarity in all situations.

yoga pose

Seated side stretch pose

questions for introspection
How balanced are your emotions? Do you find yourself leaning more toward heaviness or lightness? What intentional practices can help you bring more emotional harmony into your life?

Step Two:
Recognize any disruption in your energy flow

DAY 23

mantra
I feel empowered in my pleasure.

words of wisdom

Sex is more than physical pleasure—it is an energetic exchange that can deepen connection and awareness. When approached with intention, it becomes a transformative experience that goes beyond the surface. Be mindful of your intentions, listen to your body, and trust your intuition. True pleasure is found not only in the act, but in the depth of connection you allow yourself to experience.

yoga pose

Wide-angle seated forward bend pose

questions for introspection
How would you describe your relationship with pleasure and intimacy? Do you feel fulfilled? What can you explore to deepen your connection to pleasure in a conscious and aligned way?

DAY 24

mantra
I feel spontaneous and free.

words of wisdom

The time to act is now. Waiting creates distance between you and your desires. There is no "right time" because time itself is always aligned with Divine flow. When you take action, you activate your ideas and begin the process of manifestation. Do not delay what your soul is ready to bring into reality —start where you are and trust the unfolding.

yoga pose

Half lord of the fishes pose

questions for introspection
What ideas or projects are calling you to be created? What steps can you take today to begin bringing them into reality?

DAY 25

mantra
I feel liberated in my sexuality.

words of wisdom

There is no shame in sexual exploration. It is a natural expression of your authentic self and a gateway to deeper understanding of your being. External judgment may attempt to limit your freedom, but true liberation comes from self-acceptance. When you fully embrace all aspects of yourself, you dissolve judgment and step into your truth without fear.

yoga pose

Seated forward bend pose

questions for introspection
Are your beliefs around sexuality expansive or limiting? What experiences or conditioning may be blocking your full expression, and how can you begin to release them?

DAY 26

mantra
I feel unique and multidimensional.

words of wisdom

Your inner child once existed without limitation, freely dreaming and expressing without fear. Over time, external influences may have dimmed that light, but it has never left you. Reconnect with your original essence, reclaim your ambitions, and honor your uniqueness. You have the power to revive your highest expression and live in alignment with your true self.

yoga pose

Sphinx pose

questions for introspection
What are your true aspirations? What is currently holding you back from stepping fully into them?

DAY 27

mantra
I feel inspired by my mind and spirit.

words of wisdom

Expand beyond conventional thinking. When your mind and spirit are aligned, your vision becomes clearer and your creativity becomes more intentional. This connection allows you to access deeper parts of yourself and express your ideas with purpose and clarity. Your imagination is not random—it is a powerful force meant to be explored and expressed.

yoga pose

Cobra pose

questions for introspection
How connected are you to your creative energy? What practices are you using to nurture it, and how can you expand your creative expression?

DAY 28

mantra

I feel important and valued in the Universe.

words of wisdom

Your worth is not determined by income or social status. These are external constructs that do not define your value or your influence in the Universe. While financial stability can support your peace of mind, it should not control your identity. Stay grounded in the present moment, prepare with intention, and release fear of the uncertain future.

yoga pose

Bow pose

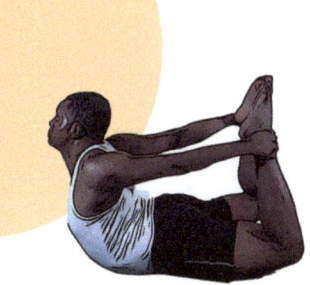

questions for introspection

Do you feel financially secure and supported? What habits or mindset shifts can help you cultivate deeper stability and flow?

DAY 29

mantra
I feel free of stress and at ease.

words of wisdom

Stress and anxiety are often rooted in fear and unconscious patterns. When you allow fear to take control, it disrupts your sense of flow and well-being. In these moments, choose awareness over reaction. Face your fears with courage, breathe through discomfort, and allow yourself to move beyond what once limited you. Growth is found in your willingness to rise above fear.

yoga pose

Eagle pose

questions for introspection
What fears are present in your life right now? How do they influence your decisions? What steps can you take to move through those fears and reclaim your power?

Solar Plexus Chakra

The solar plexus chakra is the center of self-identity, self-worth, and personal power. It governs how you see yourself, how you show up in the world, and how confidently you take ownership of your life.

When imbalanced, challenges may arise in self-esteem, confidence, trust, personal honor, and responsibility. These imbalances can also manifest physically through digestive issues, eating imbalances, and inflammation or fatigue in the body.

When balanced, the solar plexus chakra empowers confidence, clarity, and inner strength. You move with purpose, self-respect, and a calm, grounded sense of personal power that supports every aspect of your life.

As you move through the mantras and yoga poses connected to this chakra, take at least **<u>eight</u>** deep, intentional breaths—inhaling fully and exhaling with awareness to strengthen your power and restore balance.

Solar Plexus Chakra Pose Instructions

- **Wild thing pose** – from side plank, step your top foot behind you and lift your hips while reaching your top arm overhead.
- **Tiger pose** – from tabletop, lift one leg and arch your spine, then round your back and draw your knee toward your nose.
- **Warrior I pose** – step one foot forward, bend the front knee, and lift your arms overhead with hips facing forward.
- **Revolved abdomen pose** – sit or lie on your back and twist your torso, bringing your elbow to the opposite knee or extending your arms outward.
- **Revolved wide-legged forward bend pose** – stand wide, fold forward, and twist your torso, reaching one arm upward.
- **Staff pose** – sit tall with legs extended straight and spine upright, hands resting by your sides.

Solar Plexus Chakra Pose Instructions

- **Lizard pose** – step one foot forward, lower your hips, and bring your hands or forearms to the ground inside your foot.
- **Cat pose** – from tabletop, round your spine upward and draw your chin toward your chest.
- **Wind release pose** – lie on your back and pull your knees into your chest, hugging them in.
- **Downward facing dog pose** – lift your hips up and back, forming an inverted V-shape with your body.
- **Upward plank pose** – sit, press into your hands and feet, and lift your hips to form a straight line.
- **Boat pose** – balance on your sit bones, lift your legs, and extend your arms forward.
- **Half lotus tree pose** – stand on one leg, place the opposite foot on your thigh, and bring hands to center or overhead.
- **Extended mountain pose with backbend** – stand tall, reach your arms overhead, and gently arch your upper body back while keeping your core engaged.

DAY 30

mantra

I do embody full capability, allowing courage to flow through my body.

words of wisdom

Accountability is the foundation of your personal power. To fully realize your potential, you must take ownership of your actions, thoughts, and decisions. It may feel easier to shift responsibility onto others, but true growth begins when you look within. When you choose courage over blame, you release yourself from the weight of the past and step into self-mastery. Your liberation begins the moment you accept your role in your own evolution.

yoga pose

Wild thing pose

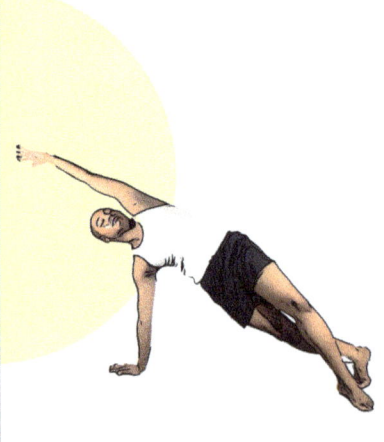

questions for introspection

Do you hold yourself accountable for your actions? In what areas of your life do you fully take responsibility, and where do you tend to shift it? How can you strengthen your commitment to self-accountability?

DAY 31

mantra

I do remain present in my growth, unattached to past or future.

words of wisdom

Do not define yourself by others' perceptions. External opinions are projections, not truths. When you attach your identity to how others see you, you disconnect from your authentic self. Release the need to prove your worth and begin validating yourself from within. You are already whole, already powerful, and already enough. When you stand firmly in who you are, your soul experiences true freedom.

yoga pose

Tiger pose

questions for introspection

Do you validate yourself from within, or do you rely on external approval? What recognition or validation did you lack growing up, and how can you now give that to yourself consistently?

DAY 32

mantra

I do trust my choices with confidence and inner clarity.

words of wisdom

Own your choices with confidence and intention. Every decision you make contributes to your growth and expansion. What may appear as mistakes are simply lessons guiding you forward. Trust that your path is unfolding exactly as it should. When you move without fear and align your actions with your purpose, you strengthen your connection to your inner authority.

yoga pose

Warrior I pose

questions for introspection

What practices support your personal growth and transformation? Are these practices aligning you with the life you truly desire? If not, what needs to shift?

DAY 33

mantra

I do pursue my ambitions with purpose and drive.

words of wisdom

Respect is an energetic exchange rooted in integrity. When you respect yourself deeply, it naturally extends to others without condition. The ego may attempt to limit respect based on judgment, but true alignment comes from honoring all beings. When you embody respect in your actions and words, you elevate your presence and reinforce your character.

yoga pose

Revolved abdomen pose

questions for introspection

How do you define respect? Do you genuinely respect yourself, others, and the greater order of life? In what ways can you deepen your expression of respect?

DAY 34

mantra

I do maintain mental balance and inner stability.

words of wisdom

Master your inner world, for it shapes your external experience. Your mind is powerful, but it is not your master—you are. Words from others only affect you when you internalize them. Choose what you allow to enter your space. When you cultivate awareness and resolve internal tension, you maintain clarity, strength, and emotional balance.

yoga pose

Revolved wide-legged forward bend pose

questions for introspection

How open are you to receiving feedback? Do you take things personally, or can you listen with awareness? What steps can you take to receive input with clarity and without emotional attachment?

DAY 35

mantra

I do honor my inner voice above outside opinions.

words of wisdom

Unconditional love transforms your perception. The ego thrives on judgment, separation, and negativity, often shaped by past conditioning. When you rise above these patterns and choose love, you expand your awareness and reconnect with truth. Love dissolves limitation and allows you to move through life with compassion and strength.

yoga pose

Staff pose

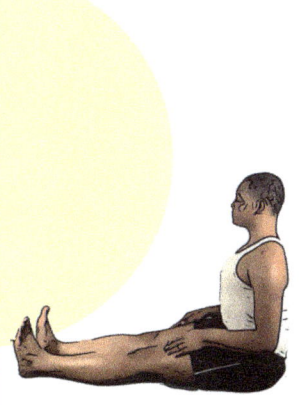

questions for introspection

In what ways do you judge yourself—your mind, body, or spirit? Do you judge others? Where did these patterns begin, and how can you begin practicing non-judgment and compassion?

DAY 36

mantra
I do rise above the ego, grounded in my true self.

words of wisdom

Be your greatest supporter. Confidence is not built from external validation but from your internal belief in yourself. The ego may try to diminish your light by comparison, but your essence is incomparable. Recognize your value, uplift yourself, and allow your presence to radiate without hesitation. Your light is meant to be seen.

yoga pose

Lizard pose

questions for introspection
How would you describe your self-esteem? Do you feel confident and secure in who you are? What can you do daily to strengthen your self-worth and inner confidence?

DAY 37

mantra
I do radiate Divine energy from within.

words of wisdom

Trust your intuition fully. Second-guessing weakens your connection to your inner guidance and creates unnecessary doubt. Your intuition is a direct extension of your Divine awareness—clear, supportive, and always aligned with your highest good. When you trust it, you move with certainty and purpose.

yoga pose

Cat pose

questions for introspection
Do you often doubt yourself or hesitate before taking action? What is the root of this hesitation, and how can you begin to trust your power more fully?

DAY 38

mantra
I do celebrate all that I have achieved in life.

words of wisdom

Your purpose is significant, regardless of how it appears. There is no hierarchy in purpose—every role contributes to the balance of the Universe. Every experience you have lived has led you to this moment of awareness. Honor your journey, appreciate your growth, and continue to evolve with gratitude.

yoga pose

Wind release pose

questions for introspection
What do you truly desire to achieve in your life? Are your current actions aligned with that vision? If not, what is holding you back from stepping into it?

DAY 39

mantra
I do release negative energy and rest in peace.

words of wisdom

Choose elevation over negativity. You have the power to shape your environment and your experience through conscious choice. Remaining in pessimistic patterns limits your growth and keeps you disconnected from your potential. Step beyond comfort, raise your frequency, and align with energy that supports expansion and possibility.

yoga pose

Downward facing dog pose

questions for introspection
Do you feel surrounded by negative or draining energy? What is preventing you from removing yourself or setting boundaries within these environments?

DAY 40

mantra

I do stand in my power and uplift others.

words of wisdom

Your energy reflects your self-perception. The vibration you carry reveals how you see yourself and what you believe you deserve. When you embody confidence and self-worth, it becomes evident in your presence. Explore the depth of who you are and embrace your wholeness without fear.

yoga pose

Upward plank pose

questions for introspection

How would you describe yourself as a multidimensional being? What unique quality defines you, and how can you begin to share and express it more openly?

Step Three:
Observe the disruption

DAY 41

mantra
I do guide and direct my thoughts with intention.

words of wisdom

Do not lose yourself in constant doing. Overworking and distraction can become ways to avoid inner awareness. Take time to pause, reflect, and observe your thoughts and emotions. When you create space for stillness, you reconnect with clarity, intention, and purpose. Balance action with awareness.

yoga pose

Boat pose

questions for introspection
How does your work or daily responsibilities make you feel? Do you experience fulfillment and purpose, or is there a disconnect that needs to be addressed?

DAY 42

mantra
I do act with discipline and self-motivation.

words of wisdom

Discipline is a pathway to transformation. It is not restriction—it is alignment with your higher self. You are not confined to one way of being; growth comes through exploration, consistency, and courage. When you take aligned risks and remain committed to your evolution, you expand beyond limitation.

yoga pose

Half lotus tree pose

questions for introspection
Are you open to stepping outside of your comfort zone? What risks are calling you forward, and what fears are holding you back from taking them?

DAY 43

mantra

I do express intelligence with confidence and clarity.

words of wisdom

Release regret and reclaim your power. Regret keeps you anchored to the past and disconnected from the present moment. Instead of replaying what was, choose to reflect, learn, and grow. Emotional intelligence allows you to understand your decisions without judgment. Your power is always available to you now—step into it fully.

yoga pose

Extended mountain pose with backbend

questions for introspection

Do you carry regret from your past? What lessons can you extract from those experiences, and how can you shift your perspective to empower your present and future?

Heart Chakra

The heart chakra is the center of love—self-love, love for others, and love for the Universe. It governs your compassion, inner peace, joy, and the depth and quality of your relationships.

When imbalanced, disruptions may arise through grief, anger, distrust, loneliness, self-centeredness, or resistance to forgiveness. These imbalances can also manifest physically in the heart, lungs, upper back, and shoulders, reflecting a blockage in emotional flow

When balanced, the heart chakra allows unconditional love to move freely through you. You experience emotional harmony, empathy, and a deep sense of compassion for yourself and others. Love becomes your natural state, guiding your thoughts, actions, and connections.

As you move through the mantras and yoga poses connected to this chakra, take at least **two** deep, intentional breaths—inhaling fully and exhaling with awareness—to open your heart and restore balance.

Heart Chakra Pose Instructions

- **One-legged revolved mountain pose** – stand on one leg, twist your torso, and bring hands together at your chest.
- **Reverse triangle pose** – step wide, straighten your front leg, and reach one arm down your back leg while the other lifts overhead.
- **Melting heart pose** – from tabletop, walk your hands forward and lower your chest toward the floor while hips stay lifted.
- **Revolved triangle pose** – step wide, extend one hand to the opposite foot, and lift the other arm upward in a twist.
- **Wheel pose** – lie on your back, press into your hands and feet, and lift your body into a full backbend.
- **Lord of the dance pose** – balance on one leg, hold the opposite foot behind you with the same hand, and extend the leg back while lifting your chest forward.
- **Camel pose** – kneel, place hands on your heels, and lift your chest upward into a backbend.
- **Dancer's pose** – stand on one leg, hold the other foot behind you, and extend your chest and arm forward.

Heart Chakra Pose Instructions

- **Standing backbend pose** – stand tall, reach your arms overhead, and gently arch your upper body back.
- **Volcano pose** – stand with feet grounded and sweep your arms up overhead, bringing palms together.
- **Gate Pose** – kneel with one leg extended to the side and reach your arm overhead in a side stretch.
- **Bound warrior I pose** – from warrior I pose, bring your arms behind your back and clasp your hands.
- **Palm tree pose** – stand tall, lift your arms overhead, and stretch upward through your entire body.
- **Half bow pose** – lie on your belly, hold one ankle, and lift your chest and leg upward.

DAY 44

mantra

I love my connection to all beings in the Universe.

words of wisdom

Your connection to others and the Universe is strengthened through your willingness to be fully present. When you release fear of judgment and external perception, you open yourself to authentic living. True vulnerability is not weakness—it is the gateway to deeper connection. You are never separate from the whole; you are always connected. Choose openness over isolation and allow your heart to lead.

yoga pose

One-legged revolved mountain pose

questions for introspection

Do you nurture a genuine emotional connection with yourself and others? What steps can you take to become more open, honest, and vulnerable in your relationships?

DAY 45

mantra

I love creating and honoring healthy boundaries.

words of wisdom

Healthy relationships thrive where there is both freedom and boundaries. When you express yourself openly while honoring your limits, you create space for genuine connection and mutual respect. Fear-based communication weakens relationships, while soul-led communication strengthens them. Speak with intention, honor your boundaries, and be willing to release what no longer aligns with your truth.

yoga pose

Reverse triangle pose

questions for introspection

What did a healthy relationship look like to you growing up? Was this reflected in your environment? How do you now define and actively create healthy relationships within yourself and with others?

DAY 46

mantra

I love expressing compassion in all that I do.

words of wisdom

Every relationship in your life is an opportunity to deepen your understanding of connection. Whether with family, friends, or partners, your presence and participation shape the quality of that connection. When you show up with love, awareness, and intention, you cultivate compassion and strengthen your role within the interconnected web of life.

yoga pose

Melting heart pose

questions for introspection

How do your current relationships make you feel—supported, drained, inspired, or disconnected? What intentional actions can you take to cultivate more loving, balanced connections?

DAY 47

mantra
I love living in a state of eternal gratitude.

words of wisdom

Unconditional love is your natural state of being. When you place conditions on love, you limit its expression and disconnect from your true essence. Love is not meant to be controlled, restricted, or earned—it is meant to be experienced and shared freely. Release fear, remove expectations, and allow love to flow in its purest form.

yoga pose

Revolved triangle pose

questions for introspection
Do you place conditions on love? What expectations or limitations are you holding onto? How can you begin to release them and allow love to flow freely and unconditionally?

DAY 48

mantra
I love being loved and embodying love fully.

words of wisdom

Love is not defined by external standards—it is defined within you. There is no single definition of love, only the one you choose to embody and express. Take a moment to reflect on your beliefs about love. If they are rooted in conditions or expectations, release them and reconnect with love free from ego and limitation.

yoga pose

Wheel pose

questions for introspection
What does love truly mean to you? How is this definition expressed in the way you show up for yourself and others?

DAY 49

mantra
I love accepting myself and others with openness.

words of wisdom

Acceptance is the doorway to forgiveness and inner peace. When you understand that every experience serves your growth, resistance begins to dissolve. Forgiveness is not about excusing others —it is about freeing yourself from the weight of holding on. As you accept what is, you create space for healing, liberation, and emotional clarity.

yoga pose

Lord of the dance pose

questions for introspection
What does forgiveness mean to you on a deeper level? How can you begin to practice forgiveness as a form of personal liberation rather than obligation?

DAY 50

mantra
I love existing in harmony as one with myself.

words of wisdom

Your emotional energy carries immense power. It can either consume you or expand your awareness, depending on how you engage with it. When you cultivate emotional awareness and balance, you strengthen your ability to respond with intention rather than react unconsciously. Build a healthy relationship with your emotions—they are guides, not obstacles.

yoga pose

Camel pose

questions for introspection
How would you describe your current emotional health? What practices can you introduce to support greater emotional balance, awareness, and healing?

DAY 51

mantra
I love knowing I am never alone.

words of wisdom

Your pain is not your identity, but a part of your journey. Holding onto it keeps you bound to the past and delays your healing. When you choose to face your wounds with courage and compassion, you allow transformation to occur. Release the need to identify with suffering and step into renewal, growth, and emotional freedom.

yoga pose

Dancer's pose

questions for introspection
Do you hold onto your emotional wounds or identify with your pain? In what ways might this be limiting your growth, and how can you begin to release and transform it?

DAY 52

mantra

I love giving and receiving love freely.

words of wisdom

Fear can close your heart, but love itself never creates harm. It is attachment, expectation, and ego that lead to suffering. When you release these patterns, you return to the truth that love is infinite, expansive, and ever-present. Open your heart fully and allow yourself to experience love without fear.

yoga pose

Standing backbend pose

questions for introspection

How open are you to receiving love? How freely do you give it? What beliefs or experiences may be influencing your openness in both areas?

DAY 53

mantra
I love being kind and gentle with myself.

words of wisdom

Kindness begins within and radiates outward. Simple acts such as conscious breathing and genuine smiling are powerful expressions of love. When you treat yourself with compassion, you naturally extend that same energy to others. Let kindness be a daily practice—it has the power to uplift, heal, and transform your environment.

yoga pose

Volcano pose

questions for introspection
How do you treat yourself daily? Are you kind and compassionate toward your mind, body, and spirit? What intentional practices can help you deepen your self-love?

DAY 54

mantra
I love forgiving myself and others with ease.

words of wisdom

Forgiveness is a conscious act of reclaiming your power. Holding onto hurt prolongs suffering, while releasing it creates space for healing. Be patient with yourself, but do not delay your growth. When you choose forgiveness, you choose freedom, peace, and emotional renewal.

yoga pose

Gate pose

questions for introspection
Who are the people you feel called to forgive? What is holding you back from releasing that energy, and how might forgiveness create space for your healing?

DAY 55

mantra
I love devoting myself to personal transformation.

words of wisdom

Emotional trauma can shape your inner world, but it does not define who you are. When left unaddressed, it can create patterns that limit your growth. However, you have the strength and awareness to transform it. Sit with yourself, do the inner work, and allow your healing to unfold with intention and resilience.

yoga pose

Bound warrior I pose.

questions for introspection
What emotional experiences or trauma are you currently working through? Why do they still hold significance, and what daily practices can support your healing and growth?

DAY 56

mantra

I love releasing attachment in my relationships.

words of wisdom

Recognize the difference between attachment and true connection. Attachment is driven by need and control, while genuine relationships are rooted in mutual growth and shared energy. When you release attachment, you create space for relationships that uplift, expand, and support all involved.

yoga pose

Palm tree pose

questions for introspection

Which relationships in your life feel in need of healing? Why are they important to you, and what first steps can you take toward restoration or resolution?

DAY 57

mantra
I love honoring respect for myself and others.

words of wisdom

Manipulation is rooted in fear, insecurity, and a desire for control. True connection, however, is built on freedom, respect, and authenticity. When you honor your worth, you no longer accept or engage in manipulation. Stand firm in your truth, choose love, and allow your relationships to be guided by integrity and mutual respect.

yoga pose

Half bow pose

questions for introspection
Do you allow others to influence or control your emotions? How does this impact your well-being? What boundaries can you create to protect your emotional space and honor your worth?

Throat Chakra

The throat chakra is the center of self-expression, communication, and the freedom to speak your truth. It governs how openly you share your thoughts, express your creativity, and align your voice with your inner will.

When imbalanced, challenges may arise around judgment, decision-making, emotional honesty, and the confidence to pursue your dreams. These imbalances can also manifest physically in the throat, mouth, and thyroid, reflecting a blockage in authentic expression.

When balanced, the throat chakra empowers clear, confident communication. You express yourself with ease, remain present and centered, and allow your creativity and intuition to flow naturally through your voice.

As you move through the mantras and yoga poses connected to this chakra, take at least **five** deep, intentional breaths—inhaling fully and exhaling with awareness—to support clarity and restore balance.

Throat Chakra Pose Instructions

- **Plow pose** – lie on your back, lift your legs overhead, and bring your toes toward the floor behind you.
- **Shoulderstand pose** – lift your legs upward while supporting your lower back with your hands.
- **Half camel pose** – kneel, place one hand on your heel, and reach the other arm upward or back.
- **Fish pose** – lie on your back, lift your chest, and gently arch your head back.
- **Dolphin pose** – from forearms and feet, lift your hips up and back into an inverted V-shape.
- **Sage Nahusha pose** – kneel with knees wide and feet together behind you, then lean back, opening your chest and reaching toward your heels.
- **Humble warrior pose** – from warrior I pose, clasp your hands behind your back and fold your torso forward.
- **Raised legs pose** – lie on your back and lift your legs straight up toward the ceiling.
- **Bed pose** – sit or lie back, open your chest, and support your body with your arms behind you.
- **Bridge pose** – lie on your back, bend your knees, and lift your hips upward.

Throat Chakra Pose Instructions

- **One-legged shoulderstand pose (hands on back)** – lift into shoulderstand, support your back, and extend one leg upward.
- **Chair pose** – stand, bend your knees, and lift your arms overhead as if sitting back into a chair.
- **Snail pose** – from shoulderstand, bend your knees and bring them toward your ears.
- **Fierce pose** – stand grounded, bend your knees deeply, and raise your arms overhead with strength.

DAY 58

mantra
I speak as my voice of truth.

words of wisdom

Truth is liberation. When you speak from ego to gain approval, you create a false reality that disconnects you from your authentic self. These patterns may protect you from judgment in the moment, but they bind you to internal conflict. When you choose honesty, you release that weight and step into freedom. Your truth is enough—speak it with confidence, regardless of how it is received.

yoga pose

Plow pose

questions for introspection
Do you speak your truth, or do you create stories to protect your ego? In what moments do you hold back from honesty, and why?

DAY 59

mantra
I speak my feelings and thoughts with openness.

words of wisdom

Your voice may have been shaped by your environment, but it is not defined by it. Early experiences may have encouraged or suppressed your expression, and those patterns can follow you into adulthood. However, you have the power to rewrite them. Release the fear of how others will respond and begin to express yourself freely, openly, and without limitation.

yoga pose

Shoulder stand pose

questions for introspection
How clearly do you express your thoughts? Do you feel understood when you speak, or do you struggle to articulate what you truly mean?

DAY 60

mantra
I speak with intention and clarity.

words of wisdom

Your words are powerful—they shape your reality and influence your path. When you speak with intention, clarity, and truth, you align with manifestation and integrity. Honor your word as a commitment to yourself. If you feel misaligned, pause, reflect, and realign your speech with honesty and purpose.

yoga pose

Half camel pose

questions for introspection
How intentional are you with your words? Do you treat your words as commitments? In what ways have you honored—or gone back on—what you've said?

Step Four:

Surrender your hold on any negative energy flow

DAY 61

mantra
I speak with confidence and ease.

words of wisdom

Integrity is the alignment of your words and actions. When you say one thing and do another, you weaken your connection to yourself. Fear often creates this disconnect, but when you face that fear and act in alignment with your truth, you strengthen your spiritual integrity. Let your actions reflect the power of your voice.

yoga pose

Fish pose

questions for introspection
Do your actions align with your words? Where is there a disconnect, and how can you begin to move with greater integrity and intention?

DAY 62

mantra
I speak clearly and listen with presence.

words of wisdom

Balanced communication requires both expression and deep listening. When you focus only on speaking, you miss understanding. When you only listen, you silence your truth. True connection is found in the harmony of both. Be present in your conversations, open to growth, and willing to both share and receive.

yoga pose

Dolphin pose

questions for introspection
How freely do you express yourself? How deeply do you listen to others? What can you do to create balance between speaking and truly hearing?

DAY 63

mantra
I speak with awareness of my breath.

words of wisdom

Your breath is the anchor of your voice. Mindful breathing grounds your thoughts, calms your body, and brings clarity to your speech. When you become aware of your breath during communication, you gain control over your energy and presence. Allow yourself to pause, breathe deeply, and release any tension before you speak.

yoga pose

Sage Nahusha pose

questions for introspection
What happens in your body when you try to express yourself? Do you notice tension, tightness, or hesitation? What practices can help you release this and speak with ease?

DAY 64

mantra
I speak from Divine thought and wisdom.

words of wisdom

You are a channel for wisdom and Divine insight. When you are open and aware, you receive guidance that elevates your consciousness and supports your growth. Do not overlook these moments of clarity. Stay present, listen deeply, and allow wisdom to move through you and into your expression.

yoga pose

Humble warrior pose

questions for introspection
How often do you listen to your inner guidance? Are you open to receiving wisdom from others without resistance? How do you discern what aligns with your truth?

DAY 65

mantra
I speak as my authentic self in the Universe.

words of wisdom

Authenticity amplifies your voice. When you dim your truth to fit into environments or meet expectations, you disconnect from your power. You are the source of your own comfort and acceptance. Release the need for external validation and allow your authentic self to be expressed in every space you enter.

yoga pose

Raised legs pose

questions for introspection
Do you feel comfortable being your authentic self in all environments? Where do you hold back, and what would it take to fully show up as you are?

DAY 66

mantra
I speak calmly, free from anxiety.

words of wisdom

Stillness creates clarity in your speech. Anxiety often arises from internal noise and a resistance to silence. When you avoid stillness, your words become rushed and ungrounded. Embrace quiet moments, cultivate inner peace, and allow your voice to emerge from a place of calm and centered awareness.

yoga pose

Bed pose

questions for introspection
How do you feel about silence? Do you avoid it or embrace it? What practices can help you create more stillness in your inner and outer world?

DAY 67

mantra
I speak with kindness and care.

words of wisdom

Speak with kindness and conscious intention. The past does not define your voice in this moment. Each word you choose has the power to uplift or diminish. Choose language that brings light, encourages growth, and reflects compassion for yourself and others.

yoga pose

Bridge pose

questions for introspection
What does your inner child need to hear from you right now? What truths or wisdom are you ready to express and share with the world?

DAY 68

mantra
I speak while listening deeply to myself and others.

words of wisdom

Listen to yourself with honesty and depth. Avoiding your inner truth limits your growth and self-awareness. When you create space to reflect—through journaling, stillness, or mindful observation—you strengthen your connection to your inner voice. The more you listen to yourself, the more you understand others.

yoga pose

One-legged shoulderstand pose (hands on back) pose

questions for introspection
Do you create space for honest self-expression through journaling or reflection? When you write, are you fully truthful and free of judgment? How can you deepen this practice?

DAY 69

mantra
I speak knowing I am worthy of being heard.

words of wisdom

Your voice deserves to be heard, but it does not need to be forced. The need for constant validation often stems from past experiences where your voice was not valued. Release this attachment and understand that communication is an exchange, not a competition. Speak from a place of healing, not from a need to be recognized.

yoga pose

Chair pose

questions for introspection
Do you ever feel unheard or overlooked in conversation? What beliefs or patterns may be contributing to this, and how can you communicate more effectively and confidently?

DAY 70

mantra
I speak with independence and self-trust.

words of wisdom

Protect your voice and your truth. Do not give your power away to fear, insecurity, or conditioning. Your perspective is unique and meaningful. When you stand firmly in your truth and trust your inner authority, you reclaim ownership of your voice and your expression.

yoga pose

Snail pose

questions for introspection
Do you allow anyone to have power over your voice? Why? What steps can you take to reclaim ownership of your expression and truth?

DAY 71

mantra
I speak as a voice of love.

words of wisdom

Conscious communication creates harmony and connection. When you understand your communication style and remain open to others, you create an environment of respect and growth. Every voice holds value. Speak with love, listen with intention, and allow your interactions to be guided by awareness and mutual understanding.

yoga pose

Fierce pose

questions for introspection
Is miscommunication a pattern in your relationships? What intentional changes can you make to improve clarity, understanding, and connection?

Third Eye Chakra

The third eye chakra is the center of awareness, intuition, and inner wisdom. It governs your ability to see beyond illusion, access clarity, and trust your inner guidance. Your imagination, insight, critical thinking, and perception all flow through this energy center.

When imbalanced, challenges may arise in openness to the world around you, acceptance of truth, decision-making, and the ability to learn from experience. These imbalances can also manifest physically through tension in the eyes or sinuses, reflecting a lack of energetic clarity.

When balanced, the third eye chakra allows you to move with vision and awareness. You see beyond material illusion, trust your intuition, and align with self-mastery. Your perspective expands, your insight deepens, and your presence naturally inspires others.

As you move through the mantras and yoga poses connected to this chakra, take at least **<u>seven</u>** deep, intentional breaths—inhaling fully and exhaling with awareness—to enhance clarity and restore balance.

Third Eye Chakra Pose Instructions

- **Turbo dog pose** – from downward dog, bend your knees slightly and shift your weight forward and back with control.
- **Wall shoulderstand pose** – lie on your back near a wall and lift your legs up, supporting your hips with your hands or the wall.
- **Standing yoga seal pose** – stand, clasp your hands behind your back, and fold forward, lifting your arms overhead.
- **One-legged inverted staff pose** – balance on your hands, lift your body, and extend one leg upward while the other stays lifted.
- **One-legged dolphin pose** – from dolphin pose, lift one leg straight up while keeping your forearms grounded.
- **Dangling pose** – stand and fold forward, letting your head, neck, and arms hang freely.
- **Head-to-knee pose** – sit, extend one leg, and fold forward over it while the other foot rests inward.
- **Psychic union pose** – sit in lotus pose, fold forward, and bind your hands behind your back while lowering your torso.

Third Eye Chakra Pose Instructions

- **Revolved bound triangle pose** – step wide, twist your torso, bind your arms, and extend upward through your chest.
- **Thunderbolt pose** – kneel and sit back on your heels with a tall, steady spine.
- **Equal angle pose** – sit tall, bring the soles of your feet together, and allow your knees to open outward.
- **Half tortoise pose** – kneel, reach your arms forward, and lower your forehead toward the floor.
- **Lion pose** – sit tall, open your mouth wide, extend your tongue, and exhale strongly.
- **Extended puppy pose** – from tabletop, walk your hands forward and lower your chest toward the ground while hips stay lifted.

DAY 72

mantra

I see my connection to spirit with awakened consciousness.

words of wisdom

Conscious beliefs are the foundation of your awareness and energetic renewal. When you align with truths such as limitless possibility, Divine order, stillness, gratitude, and love without fear, you rise beyond ego-based thinking. These beliefs are not temporary ideas—they are a way of living and perceiving reality. When practiced consistently, they expand your vision, elevate your consciousness, and strengthen your connection to truth and inner knowing.

yoga pose

Turbo dog pose

questions for introspection

What beliefs are currently guiding your transformation? Which of these beliefs empower your growth, and which may be ready to evolve?

DAY 73

mantra

I see with insight and limitless imagination.

words of wisdom

Do not allow external forces to limit the vastness of your mind. Your perception has the ability to expand infinitely when you engage your full awareness. The ego introduces doubt, distraction, and fear to keep you confined to a narrow perspective. When you become aware of negative thought patterns and consciously release them, you step into empowerment and open yourself to deeper levels of understanding and perception.

yoga pose

Wall shoulderstand pose

questions for introspection

In what ways do you limit your own potential? Where do fear or doubt hold you back from fully expressing your limitless nature? How can you consciously shift into empowering energy?

DAY 74

mantra
I see new visions unfolding for my life.

words of wisdom

Change is constant, inevitable, and always working in your favor. Every version of yourself has purpose and belongs in the unfolding of your life. Fear of change often comes from attachment to comfort and the unknown future. When you release expectation and surrender to the present moment, you begin to see change as an ally rather than a threat. Growth lives within your willingness to evolve.

yoga pose

Standing yoga seal pose

questions for introspection
How do you respond to change? Do you resist or embrace it? What fears are attached to change, and how can you begin to trust the process of transformation?

DAY 75

mantra
I see the answers within me with clarity.

words of wisdom

Turn inward and observe your inner world with intention. When you close your eyes and become aware of your energy, you begin to notice the flow of thoughts and sensations within you. The mind may attempt to overwhelm you with questions, but stillness creates space for clarity. In stillness, you move from confusion to understanding, and your inner vision becomes more defined and aligned.

yoga pose

One-legged inverted staff pose

questions for introspection
What messages or signs have you been receiving from the Universe? What questions are you seeking answers to, and how can you turn inward to access that wisdom?

DAY 76

mantra
I see beyond illusions with truth and awareness.

words of wisdom

Your intuition reveals truth beyond illusion and surface perception. It is your internal guidance system, always working in alignment with your highest good. When you ignore it, confusion and doubt arise. The ego may attempt to rationalize or override your intuition, but your inner knowing remains steady and clear. Trust it fully—it sees what the mind cannot comprehend.

yoga pose

One-legged dolphin pose

questions for introspection
Do you experience moments of inner knowing before things unfold? How aware are you of your body's signals and your energetic responses to people and environments?

DAY 77

mantra
I see myself as the owner of my vision.

words of wisdom

Your perception shapes the reality you experience. When you focus on negativity, it becomes your lens. When you choose to see through light and possibility, your world begins to transform. You are the creator of your perception, and your life reflects the energy you consistently hold. Choose thoughts that uplift, expand, and align with your highest vision.

yoga pose

Dangling pose

questions for introspection
Do you tend to focus more on negative energy in others? What past experiences may have shaped this perception? How can you begin to see balance, light, and truth in all beings?

DAY 78

mantra
I see my intuition as a trusted guide.

words of wisdom

Your intuition is the voice of your spirit—pure, egoless, and aligned with truth. While the ego may create noise and distraction, your intuition remains grounded and direct. Strengthening your relationship with this inner voice allows you to navigate life with clarity and confidence. Listen closely, trust deeply, and act in alignment with its guidance.

yoga pose

Head-to-knee pose

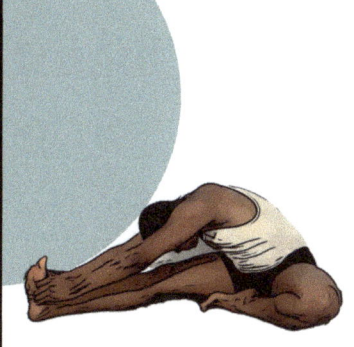

questions for introspection
How strong is your connection to your intuition? Do you trust it, or do you ignore it? What causes you to override your inner knowing?

Step Five:
Affirm high-frequency energy in your life

DAY 79

mantra
I see alignment with my higher self.

words of wisdom

A strong connection to your intuition deepens your relationship with the Universe. Your inner knowing is not separate from universal wisdom—it is an extension of it. When you trust your intuition, you align with a greater intelligence that supports your growth and evolution. Disconnection occurs when doubt takes over, so return to trust and strengthen this sacred connection.

yoga pose

Psychic union pose

questions for introspection
What is your relationship with your intuition today? What practices can you commit to that will strengthen your trust and deepen your connection to it?

DAY 80

mantra
I see Divine guidance leading my path.

words of wisdom

Break free from unconscious patterns and illusions. The ego thrives in distraction, deception, and misalignment, keeping you unaware of your true power. Awareness dissolves these illusions. When you choose conscious movement and intentional living, you reclaim control and step into a path of enlightenment and clarity.

yoga pose

Revolved bound triangle pose

questions for introspection
How present and aware are you in your daily life? In what moments do you become unconscious or distracted? How can you bring more awareness into your everyday experience?

DAY 81

mantra
I see myself as the creator of my reality.

words of wisdom

Reflect deeply on your relationships with yourself and others. Every interaction is influenced by the energy you carry and the awareness you bring. Through reflection, you gain insight into your patterns, your influence, and your role within these connections. Take accountability for your energy and intentionally create relationships that align with your truth and growth.

yoga pose

Thunderbolt pose

questions for introspection
What patterns of negative energy do you notice in your relationship with yourself and others? What steps can you take now to break these cycles and shift your energy?

DAY 82

mantra
I see through inner and universal wisdom.

words of wisdom

Deep thinking is a powerful tool for transformation. When you allow yourself to explore your thoughts with intention, you access deeper layers of awareness and understanding. This process supports healing, integration, and expansion. Your inner wisdom is always available—make time to engage with it and allow it to guide your evolution.

yoga pose

Equal angle pose

questions for introspection
How often do you create space for deep thinking and reflection? What outlets do you use to process your thoughts and gain clarity?

DAY 83

mantra
I see clarity in all my decisions.

words of wisdom

There is peace in accepting your journey exactly as it is. Every decision you have made has led you to this moment of awareness and growth. Regret is an illusion that disconnects you from trust in yourself. When you accept your past without judgment, you create space for transformation, transcendence, and inner peace.

yoga pose

Half tortoise pose

questions for introspection
Can you observe your life from a neutral perspective? How have your choices shaped your current reality? Do you see alignment with a greater purpose or Divine order?

DAY 84

mantra
I see strength in all my abilities.

words of wisdom

Consciousness restores balance within your energy and your environment. Unconscious patterns introduce negativity and disruption, but awareness allows you to recognize and release what does not serve you. You have the power to manage your energetic flow and protect your space. Stay present, observe your thoughts, and choose what you allow into your reality.

yoga pose

Lion pose

questions for introspection
In what ways do you allow negative energy to enter or remain in your life? Why do you hold onto it, and how can you begin to release it?

DAY 85

mantra
I see fear dissolve in Divine light.

words of wisdom

Illusion fades where love and awareness are present. While the ego may lead you into fantasy and distorted perception, love grounds you in truth. You were born with light, though it may have dimmed through unconscious living. Reawaken your awareness, reconnect with love, and allow your authentic vision to guide your life forward.

yoga pose

Extended puppy pose

questions for introspection
Is your life aligned with the vision you once had for yourself? If not, what has shifted, and what can you do now to reconnect with your highest vision?

Crown Chakra

The crown chakra is the center of enlightenment, inspiration, faith, and spiritual connection. It governs your awareness of the Divine, your sense of purpose, and your ability to experience inner peace, selflessness, and lasting fulfillment.

When imbalanced, challenges may arise in your values, perspective, and connection to your higher self. You may feel disconnected or resistant to seeing the bigger picture. These imbalances can also manifest as exhaustion, sensitivity to light and sound, or mental fatigue.

When balanced, the crown chakra opens you to higher consciousness and alignment. You move with trust, clarity, and a positive outlook, embracing transformation while remaining connected to the Divine and your inner truth. You heal within and extend it outward.

As you move through the mantras and yoga poses connected to this chakra, take at least **four** deep, intentional breaths—inhaling fully and exhaling with awareness—to deepen your connection and restore balance.

Crown Chakra Pose Instructions

- **Half forward fold (hands on floor) pose** – stand, hinge forward, and place your hands on the floor while keeping a slight bend in your knees.
- **Lotus pose** – sit cross-legged with each foot resting on the opposite thigh and your spine tall.
- **Rising standing cobra pose** – stand tall, lift your chest, and gently arch your upper body back with arms reaching behind or overhead.
- **Standing splits pose at wall** – stand facing down, lift one leg up against the wall, and fold your torso toward your standing leg.
- **Pyramid pose** – step one foot forward, keep both legs straight, and fold over your front leg.
- **Pendulum pose** – bend forward, place your hands behind your head, and gently swing your torso between your knees.
- **Toppling tree pose** – from Tree Pose, hinge forward while extending your lifted leg back.
- **Rabbit pose** – kneel, tuck your chin, and round your spine while placing your head toward the floor.

Crown Chakra Pose Instructions

- **Corpse pose** – lie flat on your back with arms and legs relaxed, allowing your body to fully rest.
- **Pentacle pose** – lie flat with arms and legs spread wide, forming a star shape with your body.
- **Crocodile pose** – lie on your belly, rest your head on your hands, and relax your body.
- **Half handstand pose at wall** – place your hands on the ground and walk your feet up the wall until your body forms an L-shape.
- **King pigeon pose** – from pigeon pose, bend your back leg, reach back to hold your foot, and lift your chest upward.
- **Little thunderbolt pose** – kneel, sit back on your heels, and gently lean back while keeping your spine supported.

DAY 86

mantra
I know I am releasing all that no longer serves me.

words of wisdom

Clearing your space is an act of spiritual renewal. When you release what no longer serves you—physically, mentally, and energetically—you create room for light, clarity, and alignment. Clutter reflects inner resistance. Let go of ego-driven thoughts, negative habits, and draining influences. In a clear space, your energy flows freely and your connection to higher consciousness strengthens.

yoga pose

Half forward fold (hands on floor) pose

questions for introspection
How do you intentionally clear your space—physically, mentally, and spiritually—to receive higher energy? What practices help you release what no longer serves you?

DAY 87

mantra
I know I am enlightened in my awareness.

words of wisdom

Learning is infinite and exists beyond structured environments. While external knowledge has value, your deepest wisdom comes from within. Each day presents an opportunity to understand yourself on a deeper level. When you explore your mind, body, and spirit with awareness, you unlock a level of insight that external learning cannot provide. True power is found in self-knowledge and conscious awareness.

yoga pose

Lotus pose

questions for introspection
In what ways do you invest in your self-education and inner growth? How have these practices expanded your awareness and strengthened your spirit?

DAY 88

mantra

I know my connection to spiritual and Universal energy.

words of wisdom

You are spiritually connected to all beings through the Divine. This connection is strengthened through your relationship with higher consciousness. As you grow, your understanding of this relationship evolves, guiding you through both clarity and challenge. Even in moments of darkness, the Divine remains present, offering support and balance. When you reconnect with this light, you restore your energy and realign with your true nature.

yoga pose

Rising standing cobra pose

questions for introspection

What is your current relationship with God, the Divine, or your Higher Order? How has this relationship evolved over time, and how can you deepen this connection?

DAY 89

mantra
I know I am worthy of Divine energy.

words of wisdom

Divine light is truth, and it has the power to dissolve illusion. The unconscious mind may resist this light, as it disrupts patterns of comfort and familiarity. However, remaining in darkness only prolongs disconnection and suffering. Your natural state is one of joy, clarity, and alignment. When you embrace Divine light fully, you transcend limitation and reconnect with your highest self.

yoga pose

Standing splits pose at wall

questions for introspection
Do you feel a connection with a Higher Order is important in your life? How might strengthening this relationship support your spiritual awakening and alignment?

DAY 90

mantra
I know eternal happiness lives within me.

words of wisdom

Self-care is essential for maintaining energetic balance. When any part of your being—mind, body, or spirit—is neglected, your energy becomes distorted and misaligned. A holistic approach to self-care ensures that all aspects of your existence are nurtured. Taking time for yourself is not a luxury—it is a necessity. When you prioritize your well-being, you strengthen your connection to peace, clarity, and fulfillment.

yoga pose

Pyramid pose

questions for introspection
What self-care practices do you currently honor? Are they a true priority in your life? If not, what boundaries can you create to protect and nurture your well-being?

DAY 91

mantra
I know I am whole, complete, and one with the Universe.

words of wisdom

You are whole, complete, and fully integrated within the Universe. The ego may attempt to create a sense of separation or lack, but this is an illusion. Your true nature is unity. Your mind, body, and spirit function as one, connected to the greater whole. When you move through life with this awareness, you experience deeper peace, confidence, and alignment.

yoga pose

Pendulum pose

questions for introspection
Do you feel connected to yourself and to the Universe as a whole? What can you do to deepen this sense of oneness and unity?

DAY 92

mantra
I know I am limitless and boundless.

words of wisdom

Intentional prayer is a powerful bridge between you and the Divine. When you speak with sincerity, openness, and clarity, you invite guidance, healing, and understanding into your life. Prayer is not about asking—it is about connecting. Allow your spirit to guide your words and remain open to receiving what is meant for you. Through this connection, you strengthen your spiritual awareness.

yoga pose

Toppling tree pose

questions for introspection
Is prayer part of your daily life? What do you typically focus on in your prayers? How can you make your prayer practice more intentional, open, and spiritually aligned?

DAY 93

mantra
I know I am light and unconditional love.

words of wisdom

Peace is cultivated within your being. Serenity is not dependent on external circumstances but on your relationship with your inner world. When you release unconscious patterns and emotional resistance, you create space for stillness and clarity. This inner peace becomes a foundation that supports you through all experiences. Be intentional about nurturing your calm and protecting your energy.

yoga pose

Rabbit pose

questions for introspection
When do you feel most at peace? What creates that feeling within you? How can you begin to carry that peace into your everyday life?

DAY 94

mantra
I know my spiritual insight is present and guiding me.

words of wisdom

Your thoughts carry the power to shape your reality. When influenced by unconscious patterns, they can create limitation and darkness. When guided by love and awareness, they bring clarity and expansion. Your spirit naturally aligns with truth—allow your thoughts to reflect that alignment. Choose perspectives that uplift, empower, and support your highest self.

yoga pose

Corpse pose

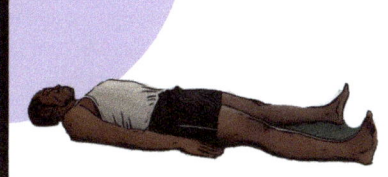

questions for introspection
Are you able to distinguish between your thoughts and your reality? In what ways might your thoughts create illusion or distortion? How can you ground yourself in truth and present awareness?

DAY 95

mantra
I know I am in harmony with my Divine purpose.

words of wisdom

Everything unfolds in Divine order, even when it is not immediately understood. Acceptance of this truth brings a deep sense of peace and trust. Your purpose is not random—it is revealed through your awareness and willingness to align with it. Release blame and resistance, and begin to see every experience as part of your evolution and spiritual growth.

yoga pose

Pentacle pose

questions for introspection
Do you ever place blame on a Higher Order for events in your life? What beliefs are behind this response, and how can you shift toward trust and acceptance?

DAY 96

mantra
I know I am a Divine being within the Universe.

words of wisdom

Your dreams are gateways to deeper awareness and understanding. They reveal insights about your mental, emotional, and spiritual state. When you pay attention to your dreams, you gain access to messages that may not surface in your waking life. Reflect on them with intention, and allow your intuition to guide your interpretation.

yoga pose

Crocodile pose

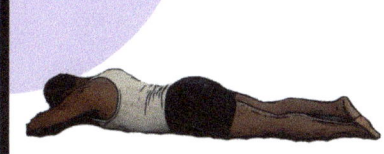

questions for introspection
What patterns or messages appear in your dreams? Do they reveal anything about your inner world, emotions, or spiritual state? How can you begin to understand and learn from them?

DAY 97

mantra
I know I am perfectly integrated and guided by the Divine.

words of wisdom

Fear is an illusion that separates you from truth and alignment. It can prevent you from embracing healthy habits and living fully in your light. When you connect with Divine energy, fear begins to dissolve. Trust in this connection and allow it to guide your healing. You are supported, protected, and capable of moving beyond fear.

yoga pose

Half handstand pose at wall

questions for introspection
What truths do you already know but have not fully integrated into your life? What steps can you take to begin living in alignment with this wisdom?

DAY 98

mantra
I know I am reunited with my spirit.

words of wisdom

True beauty is found within the soul. Physical appearance is temporary, but the essence of who you are is eternal. When you align with your inner being, your energy radiates outward in a way that cannot be replicated or diminished. This frequency of beauty is felt deeply by others. Honor your spirit and allow it to shine without limitation.

yoga pose

King pigeon pose

questions for introspection
What qualities make your spirit unique and beautiful? In what ways do others feel your energy, and how can you continue to embody that essence fully?

DAY 99

mantra
I know I am aligned with my higher self.

words of wisdom

Meditation is a transformative practice that brings you into stillness and awareness. It quiets the noise of the mind and reconnects you with your true essence. Through meditation, you gain clarity, balance, and a deeper understanding of yourself. There is no single way to meditate—explore practices that resonate with your being. Consistency in stillness leads to lasting peace and spiritual alignment.

yoga pose

Little thunderbolt pose

questions for introspection
Do you have a meditation practice? How do you ground yourself during meditation? What can you do to deepen your consistency and connection to this experience?

Closing

You have completed this journey—and in doing so, you have returned closer to yourself. Take a moment to acknowledge your commitment, your reflection, and your willingness to grow. If you have moved through this process with intention, you may now feel a greater sense of lightness, clarity, and alignment within your spirit.

Through your practice, you have strengthened your awareness and cultivated a healthier internal dialogue. This integration—reflection paired with intentional action—is where true transformation lives. The more present you become, the more your awareness expands, and the more empowered you are to move with purpose. You are now equipped to recognize, navigate, and protect your energy with confidence and clarity.

The balance of your chakras is essential to your energetic frequency. As a spiritual being, you are naturally attuned to energy—you can feel it, sense it, and influence it. This awareness is your power. This cleanse was an invitation to release what no longer serves you and reconnect with your highest potential.

Throughout this journey, you have:
- Connected with your past, present, and future through the power of the present moment.
- Examined your fears and challenges with honesty and awareness.
- Faced those fears with courage.
- Explored your thoughts and implemented practices to rise above limitation.
- Reconnected with your truth and your light.

You are light.

When you release attachment to unconscious patterns

and begin to align with your soul and the Divine, you experience spiritual liberation. Negative energy exists at a lower frequency and can easily spread when we are unaware. But through awareness and self-protection, you elevate your energy and maintain a higher frequency. This is the foundation of a liberated mind and spirit—one that is cultivated through consistent, conscious living.

Everything is connected. Your mind, body, and spirit function as one. Without healing your inner world, your outer world cannot fully align. This cleanse is not separate from your physical well-being—it is an essential part of your total integration. When one area is neglected, imbalance follows. But when all aspects are nurtured, harmony is restored.

It is my hope that through this 99 Day Cleanse, you have experienced a meaningful shift toward balance and alignment. True well-being is found in harmony—physically, mentally, spiritually, emotionally, financially, and energetically. You now carry a renewed frequency within you. Do not contain it—allow it to flow outward into the Universe through your presence, your actions, and your truth.

As you continue forward, remember that this is not the end—it is a continuation. Your journey of awareness, healing, and expansion is ongoing. Stay present. Stay intentional. Stay connected.

I leave you with this final mantra. As you inhale and exhale, repeat:

I am connected to the present moment and the light within me.